STAR ★ FILES

Orlando Bloom

Kay Barnham

Raintree

Chicago, Illinois

Originated by Modern Age
Printed and bound in China by South China
Printing Company

10 09 08 07 06
10 9 8 7 6 5 4 3 2 1

**Library of Congress Cataloging-in-
Publication Data**
Barnham, Kay.
  Orlando Bloom / Kay Barnham.
     p. cm. -- (Star files)
  Includes bibliographical references and index.
  ISBN 1-4109-1658-8 (library binding--hardcover)
  1. Bloom, Orlando, 1977---Juvenile literature. 2.
Motion picture actors and actresses--Great Britain--
Biography--Juvenile literature. I. Title. II. Series.
  PN2598.B6394B37 2005
  791.4302'8'092--dc22

2005005253

Acknowledgments
The author and publisher are grateful to the
following for permission to reproduce copyright
material: Allstar Picture Library pp. **9** (b), **10** (l),
11, **12**, **14**, **15**, **16** (l), **16** (r), **17**, **18**, (l), **18** (r),
27, **29**, **39** (b), **40**; Corbis pp. **4**, **8**, **10** (r) (Jim
Ruymen/Reuters), **22** (b), **33** (b), **39** (t); Getty
Images pp. **6**, **30** (t), **31** (t), **31** (b), **33** (t) (Stephen
Shugerman/Stringer), **35** (l) (Jim Ross/Stringer), **35**
(r); Retna Pictures Ltd. pp. **7** (l) (Grayson
Alexander), **7** (r) (Adrian Boot), **13** (r) (Sara De
Boer), **25** (r) (Gregorio Binuya), **26** (l) (Gina
James/Graylock.com), **32** (Grayson Alexander), **37**
(Tammie Arroyo), **38** (r) (MLC), **41** (t) (John
Spellman), **43** (Ernie Stewart); Rex Features pp. **5**
(Stephen d'Antal), **9** (t) (Erik C Pendzich), **13** (l)
(New Line/Everett), **19** (Simon Runting), **20**
(Everett Collection), **21** (Focus/Everett), **22** (t)
(AXV), **23** (Universal/Everett), **24** (Walt
Disney/Everett), **25** (l) (Walt Disney/Everett), **26**
(r) (Warner Br/Everett), **28** (New Line/Everett), **30**
(b) (Eric Ford), **34** (New Line/Everett), **36** (Chris
Hatcher/BEI), **38** (l) (Charles Sykes), **41** (b) (Eric
Ford), **42** (Miramax/Everett).
Cover photograph reproduced with permission of
Corbis.

Quote sources: p. **5** www.etherealattic.co.uk;
pp. **7**, **11**, **43** *Orlando Bloom: The Biography* by
A. C. Parfitt; pp. **8**, **12**, **16**, **21**, **32**, **36**
www.theorlandobloomfiles.com; p. **10**
Ed Wilson, Artistic Director, National
Youth Theatre; p. **23** www.visimag.com;
p. **29** www.perfectpeople.net; p. **31**
www.allmovieportal.com; p. **35** interview
with Orlando Bloom on *So Graham Norton*,
March 1, 2002, Channel 4, United Kingdom;
p. **39** www.ctv.ca; p. **40** www.timesonline.co.uk.

The publishers would like to thank Sarah
Williams, Charly Rimsa, Catherine Clarke,
and Caroline Hamilton for their assistance
in the preparation of this book.

Every effort has been made to contact
copyright holders of any material reproduced in
this book. Any omissions will be rectified
in subsequent printings if notice is given to the
publishers.

The paper used to print this book comes from
sustainable resources.

Contents

Any words appearing in the text in bold, **like this**, are explained in the glossary. You can also look out for them in the Star words box at the bottom of each page.

Elf, Boxer, Pirate, Outlaw

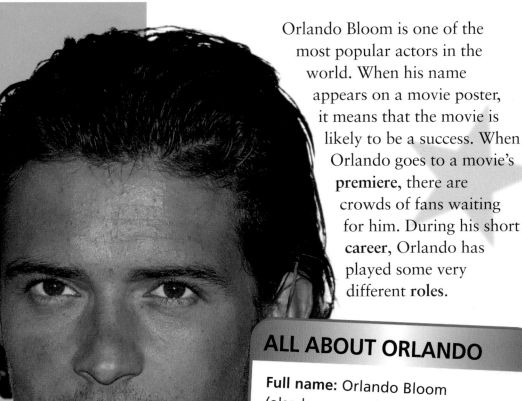

Orlando Bloom is one of the most popular actors in the world. When his name appears on a movie poster, it means that the movie is likely to be a success. When Orlando goes to a movie's **premiere**, there are crowds of fans waiting for him. During his short **career**, Orlando has played some very different **roles**.

ALL ABOUT ORLANDO

Full name: Orlando Bloom (also known as Orli or OB)
Born: January 13, 1977
Place of birth: Canterbury, Kent, England
Family: Stepfather: Harry; mother: Sonia; older sister: Samantha; birth father: Colin Stone
Height: 5 feet, 11 inches (1.8 meters)
Marital status: Single
Big break: Appearing in the movie *Wilde* in 1997
First major movie: *The Lord of the Rings: Fellowship of the Ring* (2001)
Other interests: Photography, sculpting, extreme sports such as skydiving and snowboarding

4

Star words   outlaw old-fashioned word for someone who breaks the law or who is a criminal

In *The Lord of the Rings*, he was an elf. In *Pirates of the Caribbean*, he was a pirate. He has also acted as a boxer, an **outlaw**, and a prince. Which parts will he play next? One thing is for sure: Orlando is always ready for the next challenge.

> " I've been an elf . . . a boxer, a pirate, and an outlaw. I really am living every boy's dream. "

Who did Orlando play in *The Lord of the Rings*?

What part did Orlando play in *Troy*?

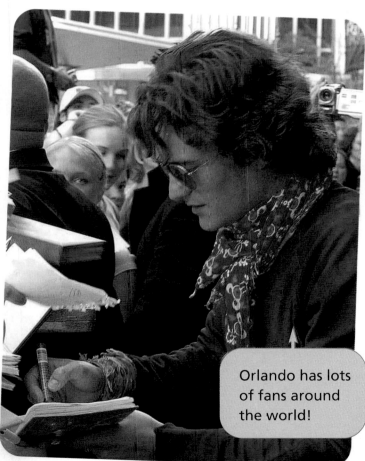

Orlando has lots of fans around the world!

In which movie does Orlando appear with Kirsten Dunst?

premiere first showing of a movie, often with celebrities invited
role part that an actor plays in a movie, play, or television show

Young Orlando

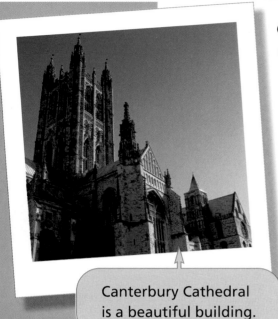

Canterbury Cathedral is a beautiful building.

Orlando Bloom was born in Canterbury. This is a small, historic city in the southeast of England. He lived there with his parents and his sister. Orlando did not have a showbusiness upbringing. He had a happy, normal childhood.

Famous father

Orlando's father was Harry Bloom. Harry was born and grew up in South Africa. He believed that the way South Africa was run was wrong, and so he spoke out against it. Black and white people were made to live apart. Black people were very poor and had very few rights. When Harry wrote novels about how wrong he felt this to be, he was thrown in prison. In 1963 he and his wife moved to England. Sadly, Harry Bloom died in 1981, when Orlando was just four years old.

A movie star's name

Orlando Bloom's real name is . . . Orlando Bloom! He is named after a 17th-century **composer** named Orlando Gibbons. Orlando's parents chose a name that everyone would remember. That is a good thing for a movie star!

★ Star fact

Orlando is not the only actor in the family. Orlando's older sister, Samantha, went to the Guildhall School of Music and Drama in London. Will Samantha be as famous as her brother in the future?

Star words   composer person who writes music

Orlando had two fathers: Harry Bloom and Colin Stone.

Harry Bloom worked with the famous African leader Nelson Mandela (see below). They were in prison together, too. Mandela was in prison for 27 years. He was finally released in 1990. He always fought for the rights of black people in South Africa. He was the country's first black president, from 1994 to 1999.

Boy with two fathers

When Orlando was thirteen years old, his mother gave him some surprising news. She told Orlando that Harry Bloom was not his real father. Orlando's father was Colin Stone. Colin had been a family friend for many years. When Harry Bloom died, Colin had become Orlando's **guardian**. Orlando was shocked by his mother's news. He kept the fact about his real father a secret for many years. Now, Orlando is pleased that he had two fathers.

"I don't know any family that doesn't have a little story somewhere."

guardian someone who is not your birth parent but who is responsible for looking after you

A creative student

When he was young, Orlando was not very interested in school. He did not want to be in a classroom. He preferred to be outside. Also, he had mild **dyslexia**. This meant he found it difficult to read.

Then, Orlando found subjects that interested him. He enjoyed studying art, sculpture, and photography. He loved drama, too.

> Don't laugh at your mates when they have problems with reading. Maybe they'll become movie stars and you'll want tickets to their premieres!

On the stage

Orlando's first taste of fame as a teenager was reading poetry at a local festival. This was good practice. Orlando soon found that speaking in front of a crowd was not at all scary. At school, he got the chance to act.

On television

As a child, Orlando's favorite television programs were *The A-Team* and *Knight Rider*. In these programs, the heroes fought against evil. Orlando wanted to be just like them.

Orlando enjoyed studying photography.

Star words   dyslexia condition in which someone finds it difficult to read

His drama teacher says that Orlando would play any **role.** He was just happy to be on stage. Orlando took part in his school's performance of *The Pirates of Penzance*. This was a musical play by the famous 19th-century British **composers** Gilbert and Sullivan.

To be a hero

Orlando loved tales of action and adventure. The *Superman* movies were his favorites. Orlando wanted to be a hero like Superman. Then, he found out that Superman was not a real person, but an actor. Orlando was surprised, but he was not disappointed. If he could not be a hero, then he would be an actor. That way, he could play the part of a hero!

Superman
Christopher Reeve (see above) was a famous actor. He starred in four *Superman* movies from 1978 to 1987. Reeve was **paralyzed** in a riding accident in 1995. He worked hard on behalf of disabled people. Sadly, he died in 2004. To many people, he was a hero on screen and a hero in real life.

Christopher Reeve starred as Superman.

paralyzed when someone cannot move a part of his or her body

9

A Star on the Rise

Orlando was determined to become an actor. When he was sixteen, he was given the chance to follow his dream. He won a **scholarship** to the National Youth Theatre in London. Orlando left Canterbury to head off to the capital city.

★ **Star fact**

When he moved to London, Orlando's favorite hobby was going out to nightclubs.

Not just acting

The National Youth Theatre teaches students all about the theater. They learn much more than just acting. There are lessons in lighting, sound, scenery, and costumes. Orlando loved his classes. One of his teachers later said, "Orlando was one of the finest young performers we've ever had."

Following the stars

Many famous actors went to the National Youth Theatre. Academy Award winner Daniel Day-Lewis studied there. You can see him in the picture above as the star of the movie *The Last of the Mohicans*. Timothy Dalton studied at the National Youth Theatre, too. He is famous for playing the part of James Bond.

Hollywood star Kevin Spacey has taught at the British American Drama Academy, where Orlando studied.

Star words

scholarship when a student is given money to help him or her afford to go to a school or college

Another scholarship

Orlando acted in lots of plays at the National Youth Theatre. A **talent scout** spotted him in one performance. It was Orlando's lucky day. He was offered another scholarship, to the British American Drama Academy. This is a very highly respected college in London. At the academy, students from around the world learn about acting on stage. They are taught by leading actors such as Sir Ben Kingsley, Kevin Spacey, and Jeremy Irons.

A TV role

Orlando got an agent. It is an agent's job to find work for an actor. Orlando soon won parts in television programs. He appeared in the popular UK hospital drama *Casualty*. Orlando played the part of a patient. He also had small parts in the drama series *Midsomer Murders* and in the comedy show *Smack the Pony*.

Orlando's favorite actors:

- Daniel Day-Lewis
- Johnny Depp
- Paul Newman
- Ed Norton

Orlando says of Johnny Depp, "Johnny's been a . . . guideline for me as a young actor."

talent scout someone who looks out for talented performers such as actors, models, or athletes

Ewan McGregor

The talented Scottish actor Ewan McGregor went to the Guildhall, like Orlando. He has starred in lots of successful movies, including *Star Wars: Episode 1—The Phantom Menace.*

A big break

When he was eighteen, Orlando continued his training at the Guildhall School of Music and Drama in London. The school teaches musicians, actors, and people who want to work in the theater. Orlando spent three enjoyable years there and earned his college degree.

> I was 22, I had two more days of drama school and it was like, 'Here! Have a **career**!' Boom!

While at the Guildhall, Orlando had his first big break. He was offered a part in *Wilde*. This was a movie about the famous 19th-century poet and **playwright** Oscar Wilde. *Wilde* starred well-known British actors Stephen Fry and Jude Law. Orlando only had a small part in the movie, but people noticed him.

Back to school

After Orlando appeared in *Wilde*, he had many more offers of work in movies and television programs. Orlando was not ready for this. He decided that it was more important to finish his training. He gained more experience by acting in lots of plays.

Ewan McGregor played the young Obi-Wan Kenobi in *Star Wars.*

Star words   audition interview for actors or musicians, where they show their skills

An even bigger break

Near the end of his time at the Guildhall, Orlando **auditioned** for Peter Jackson. He was a movie **director** from New Zealand. Then, two days before Orlando graduated from the Guildhall, something amazing happened. Orlando was offered the **role** that was to change his life. It was the part of Legolas. This was one of the main characters in *The Lord of the Rings*.

> Peter Jackson (left) chose Orlando to star in *The Lord of the Rings*.

Jude Law

One of the stars of *Wilde* was Jude Law (see above). This famous English actor has been in more than 30 movies. He has acted with Gwyneth Paltrow, Nicole Kidman, and Renée Zellweger. Perhaps he and Orlando will act together again one day . . . ?

director person in charge of making a movie

The Elf Prince

★ ★ ★ ★ ★ ★ ★ ★ ★

Tolkien's tales

The Lord of the Rings is a novel written by J. R. R. Tolkien (1892–1973). It was published in the 1950s. *The Lord of the Rings* is often said to be the most popular novel in the world. It has been translated into many languages.

★ ★ ★ ★ ★ ★ ★ ★ ★

The *Fellowship of the Ring* was the first movie of the **trilogy**.

The role of Legolas won Orlando a place in movie history. *The Lord of the Rings* movies were some of the most successful ever made. The three movies were **nominated** for 30 Academy awards. They won an amazing seventeen awards.

Adventures in Middle-earth

The Lord of the Rings is an **epic** story that is loved by readers of all ages. It is set in an **imaginary** land called Middle-earth. The main character of the story is Frodo, a hobbit. Hobbits are small creatures who look like humans with furry feet. Frodo's uncle gives him a magic ring. This ring must be destroyed before it falls into the hands of the evil Lord Sauron. If Sauron gets the ring, Middle-earth will be ruined. Frodo must take the ring to Mount Doom and throw it into the fiery volcano there. That is the only way to break Sauron's power.

14

Star words   epic long story, poem, or movie
imaginary make-believe

Peter Jackson (left) talks with actress Liv Tyler, who played Arwen.

The Fellowship of the Ring

Luckily, Frodo has eight friends to help him in his adventure. There is Gandalf the wizard. Sam, Pippin, and Merry are three hobbits. Aragorn and Boromir are humans. Gimli is a dwarf. Finally, there is the elf, Prince Legolas. This is the character that Orlando Bloom brings to life on screen. The nine characters are known as the Fellowship of the Ring.

★ Star fact

The three *The Lord of the Rings* films made almost $3 billion at box offices around the world.

The director

Peter Jackson had always loved *The Lord of the Rings*. He was delighted when he got the chance to direct the movies. Peter was given an Academy Award for Best Director in 2004. He won the award for the third movie, *The Return of the King.*

nominated chosen as one of the actors, movies, plays, etc., that might win an award

Samurai warriors

Orlando prepared well for *The Lord of the Rings*. He watched movies about **samurai** warriors. Orlando tried to act in a calm and focused way, just like them. *The Seven Samurai* (1954) is one of his favorite movies (below).

An action hero

Orlando had to spend two months training for *The Lord of the Rings*. Legolas the elf is a very athletic character. He is an expert at **archery**. He can ride a horse without a saddle. He is very good at sword fighting, too. Orlando had to practice all of these skills before filming started.

Star fact

Orlando became very good at firing arrows. He could hit paper plates that his trainers threw into the air.

Copycat

Orlando also had to learn how to move smoothly and gracefully. He watched how cats walked, ran, and jumped. Then, he tried to copy them. The next time you see the movies, watch Legolas closely. As he leaps and springs out of danger, does he remind you of a cat?

Elves are . . . graceful and elegant like cats . . . That's how I tried to be.

Star words

archery shooting using a bow and arrow. Archery is just a sport now, but it used to be an important way of fighting.

A new language

In *The Lord of the Rings*, the elves speak a language called Elvish. The language was invented by the author, J. R. R. Tolkien. Orlando and other members of the cast learned how to speak Elvish words.

Becoming an elf

Legolas Greenleaf looks very different from Orlando Bloom. This meant that Orlando had to spend hours getting ready every day. For the movie, he totally changed the way he looked. He hid his brown curly hair beneath a long, blond wig. Blue contact lenses covered his brown eyes. Orlando also wore extra-pointy elf ears!

Working with stars

Many well-known actors starred in *The Lord of the Rings* **trilogy**. Sir Ian McKellen has appeared in many movies and plays. In *The Lord of the Rings*, he plays the part of Gandalf the wizard.

Orlando learned a lot from watching Sir Ian McKellen act.

samurai warrior or soldier in ancient Japan well-known for being brave and noble

Filming in New Zealand

The Lord of the Rings movies were made in New Zealand. This beautiful country has many different types of landscapes. There are snow-topped mountains, rainforests, and **fiords**. The **director** of the movies, Peter Jackson, is from New Zealand. He thought his country was just like Middle-earth.

The movie brought lots of business to New Zealand. Many local people worked as **extras**. *The Lord of the Rings* increased New Zealand's tourism. People now visit New Zealand to see where the filming took place.

Aragorn
Viggo Mortensen (above) played Aragorn. He and Orlando became good friends off set as well as on screen. They went fishing and surfing together. Their nicknames for each other were Elf Boy and Filthy Human.

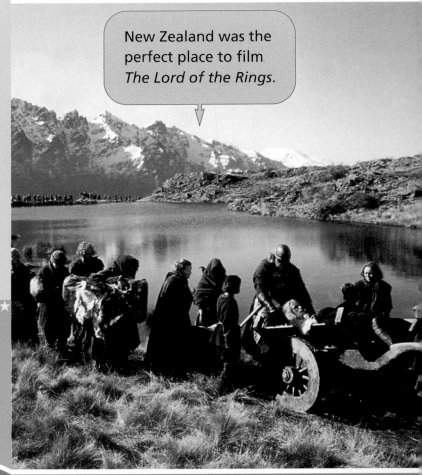

New Zealand was the perfect place to film *The Lord of the Rings*.

Star words

extra person who appears in crowd scenes in a movie. Extras are not usually given lines to speak.

The actors in *The Lord of the Rings* became close friends while they were filming.

A fellowship of actors

The Lord of the Rings movies were all made at the same time. It took eighteen months to shoot all three movies. The cast and crew lived in New Zealand while filming took place.

New Zealand is more than 11,180 miles (18,000 kilometers) away from the United Kingdom. This meant that Orlando was a long way from his home and family during filming. However, he enjoyed his time in New Zealand. Orlando became friends with his fellow actors. They had a lot of fun together.

Fellowship

Cast members were tattooed with a special symbol. This was the number nine in Tolkien's language of Elvish. They chose this symbol because there were nine members of the Fellowship of the Ring. The tattoo would remind the actors of their time in New Zealand and of their friendship.

---

fiord narrow and rocky passage of water in the sea

Lord of the Box Office

Black Hawk Down

In 2001 Orlando appeared in *Black Hawk Down*. This was a realistic war movie. It starred popular actors Josh Hartnett, Eric Bana, and Ewan McGregor. Orlando played the part of a young soldier. The movie was very successful.

When *The Lord of the Rings* came out, audiences loved it. **Directors** loved it, too. They wanted to cast Orlando in their own movies. Now, Orlando could pick which **roles** to play.

A careful choice

Orlando Bloom had played the same character in three movies. Now, he needed to show audiences that he was not just an elf in a blond wig. Orlando needed to show that he was a **versatile** actor. Orlando soon made a decision. He agreed to play an Australian **outlaw**. The movie was called *Ned Kelly*. It came out in 2003.

Orlando played the part of a young soldier in *Black Hawk Down*.

Star words

versatile a versatile actor is one who can play many different kinds of characters

Success Down Under

Ned Kelly is based on a true story. In the movie, Orlando played the part of Joe Byrne. He was a member of the Kelly Gang. These Australian outlaws took part in daring bank robberies. They lived during the 19th century. The part of Ned Kelly was played by the popular Australian actor Heath Ledger.

> It was so rewarding playing a character who was a hero in real life to so many Australians.

The movie was not a big hit. However, it was very popular in Australia, where it made almost $3.8 million. This was 86 percent of the total box office takings in Australia in 2003.

The Kelly Gang

Ned Kelly was born in 1855 in Australia. A policeman tried to arrest Ned's brother Dan, who had stolen a horse. Ned shot and injured the policeman. Then, the Kelly brothers escaped to the bush (wilderness). Two friends joined them. Their names were Joe Byrne and Steve Hart. These four men became the Kelly Gang.

Following their daring exploits, the Kelly Gang became Australian folk heros.

21

A leading role

Orlando's next movie was called *The Calcium Kid*. This was a totally new type of project for him. A big Hollywood studio did not pay for the movie. It cost over $290 million to make *The Lord of the Rings* **trilogy**. *The Calcium Kid* had a **budget** of less than $1 million.

Orlando stars as Jimmy Connelly. He is a milkman who boxes in his spare time. Then, Jimmy accidentally injures the local boxing champion. Jimmy is persuaded to take his place. The only problem is that Jimmy has to fight the world champion. . . . His friends believe he can win. They think that the calcium in the milk he drinks will make him super-strong!

 Star fact

In real life, Orlando prefers soy milk to cow's milk. Soy milk is made from soybeans.

Guest stars

Frank Bruno and Chris Eubank (above) were once world-champion boxers. Both men appeared in *The Calcium Kid*. They did not play parts, though. They played themselves.

In *The Calcium Kid*, Orlando's character loves to drink milk!

Star words budget amount of money it costs to do something

Home sweet home

For Orlando, one of the best things about *The Calcium Kid* was the location. The movie was made in South London. This meant that Orlando could live at home during filming. He enjoyed living near his friends.

A small success

The Calcium Kid was not a huge hit. However, it was very popular with Orlando's fans. He enjoyed playing a funny **role**. Orlando's comedy skills would come in handy in one of his next movies.

66 I'm very proud of this film, because it offered an opportunity for me to be a bit of a clown. 99

Orlando plays a boxer in *The Calcium Kid*.

Comedy time

The Calcium Kid did not have a lot of famous stars. For the first time, Orlando played the leading **role**. Better still, he got the chance to act in a comedy.

Johnny Depp is a very well-known actor.

Pirates ahoy!

Orlando's next part was a **swashbuckling** one. He starred in *Pirates of the Caribbean: The Curse of the Black Pearl*. In this movie, Orlando plays a **blacksmith** named Will Turner. After he finds out that his father was a famous pirate, his life changes forever.

Captain Jack Sparrow

Johnny Depp is a very experienced actor. He has starred in more than 40 movies. In *Pirates of the Caribbean: The Curse of the Black Pearl*, he plays the part of Captain Jack Sparrow. He was **nominated** for an Academy Award for the **role** in 2004.

Orlando plays a hero once again. His character discovers that it might be more fun being a pirate than a blacksmith. He fights with a sword. He swings from ships' **rigging**. He takes part in daring adventures. He also has plenty of funny moments. In the movie, it looks as if all the actors are having a great time!

Filming in the Caribbean

Much of *Pirates of the Caribbean* was filmed in the Caribbean. Outdoor scenes were shot on the Caribbean island of St. Vincent. The indoor scenes were filmed at Disney's studios in California.

Star fact

Pirates of the Caribbean was inspired by a Disney theme-park ride.

Star words   blacksmith person who makes iron tools by hand

More adventures

The movie was a big success. Its makers decided to make not one, but two **sequels.** The stars of the movie, Johnny Depp, Orlando Bloom, and Keira Knightley, all agreed to take part.

Making movies can be very expensive. Like *The Lord of the Rings* **trilogy**, the two movies were made at the same time. This saved money.

Orlando Bloom and Keira Knightley watch as Jack Sparrow escapes.

Elizabeth Swann

Keira Knightley (below) is a popular young star from England, just like Orlando. In *Pirates of the Caribbean*, she plays the part of Elizabeth Swann. Turner and Elizabeth Swann fall in love. Will they end up together . . . ?

rigging ropes that support a ship's mast and sails
swashbuckling daring and adventurous

The Trojan War

Orlando's next **role** was in the **epic** *Troy*. This came out in 2004. The movie was based on a long poem by the ancient Greek poet Homer. The movie is about the **legendary** war between the Greeks and the people of Troy.

Eric Bana and Orlando played brothers in *Troy*.

Helen of Troy

In *Troy*, German actress Diane Kruger (above) plays the part of the beautiful Helen. Diane was not always an actress. First, she was a ballet dancer. After an injury, she became a fashion model. She made her first movie in 2002. In 2004 she acted with Nicolas Cage in *National Treasure*.

Star words   complex very complicated

Orlando starred as Paris, a prince of Troy. Paris falls in love with a beautiful woman named Helen. She runs away with him. Unfortunately, Helen is already married to a Greek king. Her husband wants her back, and so the Trojan War begins . . .

A challenging role

In other movies, Orlando had played brave heroes. He was used to fighting and winning. The part of Paris was much more **complex**. Now, Orlando had to play a character who was both loved and hated. Paris could be blinded by love. He could be foolish. He could also be a coward. Orlando rose to the challenge. This was the type of meaty role he had been waiting for.

Trojan Horse

Troy has a cast of great actors. One cast member is very unique—it is a very large wooden horse! This Trojan Horse is used to smuggle Greek warriors into Troy.

Location, location, location

The story of *Troy* is set in ancient Greece. However, *Troy* was actually filmed on the island of Malta. The movie brought lots of money to the Mediterranean island. Extra scenes were shot in Mexico.

Fellow pin-ups

Orlando Bloom was not the only good-looking actor in *Troy*. He had lots of competition! Brad Pitt (above) played Achilles, a handsome warrior. Eric Bana played Paris's brave brother, Prince Hector. Eric starred in the movie *Hulk*. He and Orlando had already acted together in *Black Hawk Down*.

Danger Man!

Horsing around

When filming *The Lord of the Rings*, it was very important that Orlando did not hurt himself. Any injuries would delay filming. This would cost extra money. Unfortunately, Orlando's horse fell onto him. Orlando cracked a rib. Luckily, he was soon back in the saddle.

★ ★ ★ ★ ★

Orlando Bloom likes to take risks. He loves to do hair-raising stunts and extreme sports. Unfortunately, his activities have often landed him in trouble. He has broken his back, his ribs, his nose, both of his legs, his arm, his wrist, a finger, and a toe. He has also cracked his skull three times.

A rooftop accident

Orlando's worst accident happened in 1998. He was just 21. He tried to open a rusty door onto a roof terrace. To do this, he climbed up an outside wall. A drainpipe pulled away from the wall, and Orlando fell. He broke his back. Doctors spent hours operating on him. They fitted two plates to his **spine**. The doctors were worried that Orlando might never walk again. However, he walked out of the hospital on crutches just twelve days later.

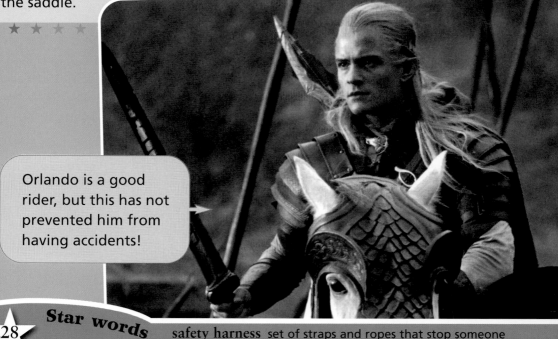

Orlando is a good rider, but this has not prevented him from having accidents!

Star words   safety harness set of straps and ropes that stop someone from falling

Getting better

It took Orlando a long time to recover from the accident. He had to wear a back brace for a year. The accident also changed him emotionally. Orlando now thinks he is more mature and more determined to succeed. His aches and pains from the accident remind him of how lucky he is to be alive. However, he still enjoys extreme sports!

> I'm rather accident-prone, I have to admit.

spine series of bones that reach from the skull to the bottom of the back

Extreme sports

Orlando loves surfing. He also enjoys white-water rafting, snowboarding, and skydiving. Orlando took part in all of these activities when he was filming in New Zealand.

He told *The Lord of the Rings* cast members that he enjoyed extreme sports. Elijah Wood (Frodo) and Viggo Mortensen (Aragorn) thought that he was joking. These sports sounded far too dangerous. It was not long before Orlando had persuaded Elijah and Viggo to come surfing with him! Soon, they learned to love the sport, too.

Orlando will jump onto a board wherever there is surf.

★ ★ ★ ★ ★ ★ ★ ★ ★ ★

Surf dude

Orlando learned to surf in New Zealand. Back home, he surfs in Cornwall, in the southwest of England. He says that the water is much colder there! Orlando still surfs with his friends from *The Lord of the Rings* whenever he can.

★ ★ ★ ★ ★ ★ ★ ★ ★ ★

Not all of Orlando's sports are extreme!

Star words
30

bungee jumping sport of leaping from a high place with a stretchy rope tied around your ankles

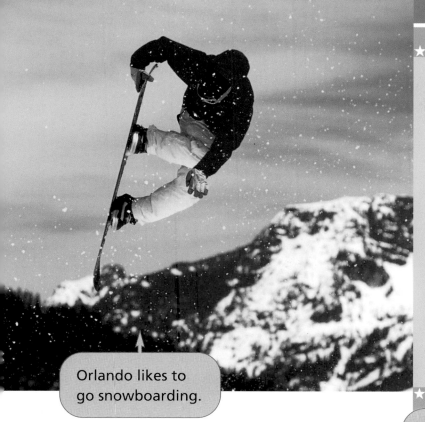

Orlando likes to go snowboarding.

Bungee jumping

The sport of bungee jumping is thousands of years old. People of the Pacific Islands still dive from wooden towers. They do not tie bungee ropes to their legs. Instead, they use vines. Boys jump to show that they have become men.

Aaaaarrrghh! Bungee jumping

New Zealand is one of the most exciting places in the world to **bungee jump**. There are many famous jumps. People jump from bridges and into canyons.

As soon as Orlando got to New Zealand, he went bungee jumping. He did not jump right away. He stood on the platform for an hour. Then, he took a deep breath and dived. Now, bungee jumping is one of his favorite sports.

> I love to . . . do kind of crazy stuff which is slightly outrageous.

Bungee jumping is now popular around the world.

Behind the Scenes

Kate's movies

Kate Bosworth made her first movie, *The Horse Whisperer,* when she was fifteen. In 2002 she starred in the surf movie *Blue Crush.* In 2004 she starred with Hollywood star Kevin Spacey in *Beyond the Sea.* She also starred in *Win a Date with Tad Hamilton.*

Orlando likes to talk about his movies, but he keeps his personal life private. You will not find Orlando talking about his love life on the pages of a celebrity magazine! He says, "I try to keep my private life separate from my **professional** life."

Orlando's girlfriends?

Orlando will not answer questions about his girlfriends, past or present. However, he and actress Kate Bosworth dated for a few years. Kate is six years younger than Orlando. She was born on January 2, 1983. Kate is from Los Angeles, California—the home of Hollywood. There were **rumors** that the couple would marry. However, they split up in 2005. They were both so busy working that they did not spend much time together.

Kate Bosworth is a popular movie star, just like Orlando.

Star words professional something related to a person's job

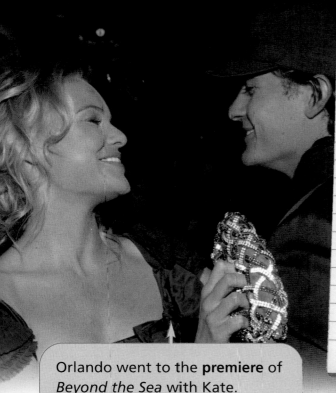

Favorite foods

Pasta

Pizza

Porridge (like oatmeal)

Rice

Spinach

Baked potatoes

Orlando went to the **premiere** of *Beyond the Sea* with Kate.

From clubbing to chilling out

When he was younger, Orlando loved to go out with his friends. He often went to nightclubs. Now, he does not have much time off. When he is not working, he prefers to relax. Orlando likes to walk along beaches. Sometimes he likes to do nothing at all!

On the move

Orlando has been in demand ever since he left drama school. He has rushed from one movie set to another. When Orlando filmed *The Lord of the Rings*, he spent eighteen months in New Zealand. He has also filmed in the United States, Australia, Malta, Mexico, and the Caribbean.

One of Orlando's favorite foods is pizza.

rumor story that lots of people discuss, but that may not be true

33

A man's best friend

Orlando loves dogs. He once owned a dog named Maude. Then, Orlando had to spend a lot of time filming in New Zealand for *The Lord of the Rings*. He was never at home to take care of his dog. Orlando gave Maude to someone who did not have to travel so much. In 2004 he and Kate Bosworth adopted two stray dogs named Siti and Guero.

A blond disguise

The Lord of the Rings made Orlando Bloom famous. Yet afterward, he found that he could still walk down the street without fans spotting him. So, why was this happening? It was all because of Legolas the elf. Many people thought that Orlando really had long blond hair and blue eyes. They did not recognize him with his dark, curly hair and brown eyes!

Fan-tastic!

Orlando now has millions of fans around the world. Every week, he receives bags of fan mail. He does not have time to reply to all of the letters. Through his fan club, he thanks everyone who has written to him.

After he starred as Legolas, Orlando's fans thought that he had blond hair, too!

Star words

technophobe someone who avoids technology, such as computers and email

Orlando was the top attraction at the 2004 Toronto International Film Festival.

Orlando does not like to let his fans down. Crowds of Orlando's fans went to the Toronto International Film Festival in September 2004. The star signed so many autographs that the showing of his new movie, *Haven*, was delayed.

Internet-free zone

Orlando Bloom does not like computers. He does not own a computer. He does not have an email address. However, Orlando's mom does like computers. She lets her famous son know of any interesting information that she finds on the Internet. Sonia Bloom at last managed to persuade Orlando to have his own official website. It went live in 2005.

I'm a technophobe.

Soccer fan

Orlando is a fan of Manchester United, the UK soccer team. He is also a fan of top soccer player David Beckham (above). Orlando supports whichever team David plays for. David now plays for the Spanish team called Real Madrid.

A true Tolkien fan

Orlando had never read *The Lord of the Rings* before he played the part of Legolas the elf. He has now read the book many times. Even after shooting three movies, this is still one of his favorite books!

A cool dresser

When he was training to be an actor, Orlando needed to earn money. He used to work in **second-hand** clothes stores. He bought his own clothes there, too. Although he could not afford much, Orlando began to develop his own style. Now, he enjoys buying the clothes he likes, no matter how much they cost.

> There was a time I could only look at the stuff in the shops, but now I can buy the outfits I really like.

Addicted to jewelry

In addition to cool clothes, Orlando loves to wear jewelry. He is often spotted wearing rings, necklaces, and watches. Look closely at photos of Orlando. He is often wearing unusual pieces of jewelry.

Orlando is a big fan of weird and wonderful jewelry.

Star words   **second-hand** something that was once owned by someone else

Favorite movies

The Hustler (1961) with Paul Newman

Stand by Me (1986) with River Phoenix

Amélie (2001) with Audrey Tautou

Orlando has a wacky sense of style. His clothes are never boring.

When Orlando was filming in New Zealand, a makeup artist gave him a special ring. It is a copy of the famous ring from *The Lord of the Rings* movies.

A sparkly present

Orlando also likes to give jewelry as presents. There are **rumors** that Orlando gave Kate Bosworth a diamond ring worth $340,000.

What's Next?

Orlando Bloom is now one of the most popular movie stars in the world. His movie **roles** are becoming more and more challenging.

A darker role

The part Orlando plays in *Haven*, which was released in 2004, is very dark. His character lives on the Cayman Islands in the Caribbean. He becomes involved with two criminals. Then, he commits a crime that affects a whole country.

Haven gave Orlando a new view of filmmaking. In addition to playing one of the main parts, he was also one of the **producers** of the movie. Like *The Calcium Kid*, *Haven* was made by a small, independent company.

Top bachelor

People is a celebrity magazine. Every year, the magazine lists Hollywood's hottest **bachelors.** In 2004 the winner was Orlando Bloom. He beat Ashton Kutcher and others to gain the top spot.

Orlando at the **premiere** of *Haven* with costar Bill Paxton (left) and the movie's **director**, Frank E. Flowers.

  Star words   bachelor man who is not married

Haven was filmed in the Cayman Islands in the Caribbean.

Famous costar

Liam Neeson stars with Orlando in *Kingdom of Heaven*. Liam is a very experienced actor. He has starred in many great movies. These include *Star Wars: Episode 1—The Phantom Menace* (see below), *Schindler's List, Rob Roy,* and *Love Actually*.

Cool outfit

Orlando really enjoyed filming *Haven*. He did not have to spend hours getting ready for his role. There were no heavy costumes. There were no wigs. Orlando did not even have to learn how to sword fight. Instead, his outfit was a pair of shorts.

It was really hot there so wearing shorts . . . was great.

From *Haven* to *Heaven*

Orlando was taken back in time once again for his next movie. *Kingdom of Heaven* is set in the 12th century. Orlando plays the part of a **blacksmith**. He protects his people against foreign invaders. The cast includes Eva Green, Liam Neeson, and Jeremy Irons. One of Orlando's all-time acting heroes, Ed Norton, also appears in the movie.

producer movie producers organize the people and money to make a movie

A life in movies

Kirsten Dunst started acting when she was three. She has appeared in more than 40 movies. At the age of twelve, she starred with Tom Cruise in *Interview with the Vampire*. Kirsten is best known for the *Spiderman* movies. She plays Mary Jane Watson, Spiderman's girlfriend.

Romance blooms

Orlando's next movie was *Elizabethtown*. This came out in 2005. Kirsten Dunst stars as Orlando's love interest. Susan Sarandon plays his mother.

Elizabethtown is a comedy-drama with a touch of romance. Orlando plays the part of a shoe designer named Drew Baylor. Drew makes a mistake that costs his company millions of dollars. Then, he is fired. Then, his girlfriend dumps him. Sadly, his father dies at the same time. Drew returns home for the funeral. He also goes to carry out his father's dying wishes. While flying home, Orlando meets a flight attendant. Suddenly, Drew's life takes a turn for the better.

> I'd love to be playing dark character roles . . . but it's about what scripts you get.

Kirsten played Mary Jane Watson, Spiderman's girlfriend.

Bond, James Bond?

In 2005 a new James Bond novel was published. The book is about James Bond's early life. There are **rumors** that there will be a movie version of the book. There are also rumors that Orlando Bloom will star as the young James Bond. Hollywood insiders say that Orlando will play the famous character before he became a secret agent. This would certainly be a treat for Orlando's fans!

Orlando enjoyed filming *Elizabethtown*. Will he enjoy playing James Bond one day?

Hollywood star

In her long **career,** Susan Sarandon (above) has acted in more than 70 movies. She has been **nominated** for four Academy awards. In 1995 she won the Best Actress award for *Dead Man Walking*. Susan keeps this award in her bathroom!

★ ★ ★ ★ ★ ★ ★ ★ ★

Hamlet

Hamlet tells the story of Prince Hamlet. His father has died and is now a ghost. The ghost tells Hamlet that his father was murdered. Hamlet does not know what to do. Is the ghost telling the truth? Should Hamlet kill the murderer?

To be or not to be?

When he was training to be an actor, Orlando appeared in many plays. Since graduating, he has spent his time in front of movie cameras. He has not appeared in any plays. However, he has said that he would love to play the part of Hamlet.

Hamlet was written by William Shakespeare. This **complex** and **tragic** tale is a very popular play. The **role** of Prince Hamlet is difficult and challenging. Perhaps this is the right part to persuade Orlando Bloom to go back on the stage?

Many famous actors have played Prince Hamlet, including Mel Gibson in a 1990 movie.

Star words   moviegoer person who goes to the movies

★ ★ ★ ★ ★ ★ ★ ★ ★

Farewell to Legolas

After *The Return of the King,* Orlando took off his elf ears for the last time. This was a very sad moment for him. Orlando had spent eighteen months being Legolas. If he had the chance, it is one part that Orlando would love to play again.

★ ★ ★ ★ ★ ★ ★ ★ ★

21st-century star

So, what does the future hold for Orlando Bloom? He has played many roles already. Hopefully, he will play a great many more. He may return to the stage. He may continue to delight **moviegoers.** There might even be an Academy Award waiting for him! Only time will tell.

> Do I want to be a pin-up? Do I want to be just a poster boy? No, I don't.

Find Out More

Books

Dougherty, Terri. *Orlando Bloom*. San Diego, Calif.: Lucent, 2005.

Kranenburg, Heather. *Lovin' Bloom*. New York: Ballantine, 2004.

Filmography

Pirates of the Caribbean 3 (2007)

Pirates of the Caribbean: Dead Man's Chest (2006)

Elizabethtown (2005)

Kingdom of Heaven (2005)

Haven (2004)

Troy (2004)

The Calcium Kid (2004)

The Lord of the Rings: The Return of the King (2003)

Ned Kelly (2003)

Pirates of the Caribbean: The Curse of the Black Pearl (2003)

The Lord of the Rings: The Two Towers (2002)

Black Hawk Down (2001)

The Lord of the Rings: The Fellowship of the Ring (2001)

Wilde (1997)

Awards

Here are just some of the many awards
Orlando Bloom has won so far:

2004 MTV Movie Awards: Sexiest Hero

2004 Screen Actors Guild Awards: Outstanding
Performance by a Cast for *The Lord of the
Rings: The Return of the King*

2003 Hollywood Film Festival Awards:
Hollywood Breakthrough Award—
Male Performer

2003 GQ Men of the Year Awards:
Best Film Actor

2003 AOL Moviegoer Awards: Best
Supporting Actor for *The Lord of the Rings:
The Two Towers*

2002 MTV Movie Awards: Best Breakthrough
Performance for *The Lord of the Rings:
The Fellowship of the Ring*

2002 Empire Awards Best Debut for *The Lord
of the Rings: The Fellowship of the Ring*

Websites

Explore the Internet to find out more about
Orlando Bloom.

There are billions of pages on the Internet, so it
can be difficult to find exactly what you are
looking for. A search engine looks through the
entire web and lists all the sites that match the
words in the search box. It can give thousands
of links, but the best matches are at the top of
the list, on the first page. Try google.com.

Glossary

archery shooting using a bow and arrow. Archery is just a sport now, but it used to be an important way of fighting.

audition interview for actors or musicians, where they show their skills

bachelor man who is not married

blacksmith person who makes iron tools by hand

budget amount of money it costs to do something

bungee jumping sport of leaping from a high place with a stretchy rope tied around your ankles

career what someone does for a job

complex very complicated

composer person who writes music

director person in charge of making a movie

dyslexia condition in which someone finds it difficult to read

epic long story, poem, or movie

extra person who appears in crowd scenes in a movie. Extras are not usually given lines to speak.

fiord narrow and rocky passage of water in the sea

guardian someone who is not your birth parent but who is responsible for looking after you

imaginary make-believe

legendary described in stories from long ago

moviegoer person who goes to movies

nominated chosen as one of the actors, movies, plays, etc., that might win an award

outlaw old-fashioned word for someone who breaks the law or who is a criminal

paralyzed when someone cannot move a part of his or her body

playwright someone who writes plays

premiere first showing of a movie, often with celebrities invited

producer movie producers organize the people and money to make a movie

professional something related to a person's job

rigging ropes that support a ship's mast and sails

role part that an actor plays in a movie, play, or television show

rumor story that lots of people discuss, but that may not be true

safety harness set of straps and ropes that stop someone from falling

samurai warrior or soldier in ancient Japan well-known for being brave and noble

scholarship when a student is given money to help him or her afford to go to a school or college

second-hand something that was once owned by someone else

sequel movie or book that continues an earlier story

spine series of bones that reach from the skull to the bottom of the back

swashbuckling daring and adventurous

talent scout someone who looks out for talented performers such as actors, models, or athletes

technophobe someone who avoids technology, such as computers and email

tragic very sad

trilogy series of three related books, plays, or movies

versatile a versatile actor is one who can play many different kinds of characters

Index